Inspired to Inspire

Copyright ©2012 by Lou E. Lambert, All Rights Reserved

Written by Lou E. Lambert
Edited and cover design by Clarissa Pace.
Shekinah Services, www.shekinahservices.com

Published and printed in the United States.

ISBN-13: 978-1478398738
ISBN-10: 1478398736

INTRODUCTION

Inspired to Inspire is a collection of inspirational sayings, quotes and scriptures compiled as a handy resource. Some of them are originals and others are quotes and scriptures that have encouraged me. Those who desire to live a victorious life and those who are fighting to rise above depression and defeat will benefit from these words of encouragement.

The devil desires to sift us as wheat. He comes to kill, to steal and to destroy. If we can control our thoughts and the words that we speak, then we can control our atmosphere.

Negativism will drain your strength while positive sayings will build you up.

My prayer is that you find the strength and the desire to make each day a better day by declaring these sayings, quotes and scriptures.

Remember, **LIFE AND DEATH** is in the power of the tongue. Be inspired to inspire.

LOU E. LAMBERT

Inspired to Inspire

Every day, let Praising God be your PRIORITY.

The First Step to Loving others is to Love yourself.

Good Warriors- Fight until the end at any cost.

Take time to make an assessment of yourself. You will probably be surprised at your self-worth.

Surround yourself with positive people, energy builds, and negativism tears down.

Inspired to Inspire

A sound Mind produces a sound Body.
A sound Body produces a sound Mind.

◊

Your life may be the only Bible others read. What are they reading?

◊

Every day is a beautiful day- Contact God to get your agenda for the rest of the week.

◊

Be strong and be of Good Courage.

◊

Waking up is the best part;
the rest is easy.

Inspired to Inspire

Pray for others during your prayer time, you will be amazed at how things began to work out for you.

◊

Be still, and know that I am God.
Psalm 46:10

◊

Lonely? Begin to show yourself friendly.

◊

S-M-I-L-E

◊

A Merry Heart doeth good like medicine: but a broken spirit drieth the bones. Proverbs 17:22

◊

LIVE to LOVE and LOVE to LIVE.

Inspired to Inspire

I can and I will

◊

DON'T COUNT ME OUT

◊

IF I DON'T GET YOU IN THE WASH - I WILL GET YOU IN THE RISE

◊

PRAY, **pray,** pray

◊

I WILL BLESS THE LORD AT ALL TIMES.

◊

HEAR ALL YOU CAN, BUT DON'T CAN ALL YOU HEAR

Inspired to Inspire

YOU SET THE TONE FOR THE DAY- SPEAK TO
THE ATMOSPHERE AND DECLARE
THAT THIS IS A GOOD DAY!

◊

You are a child of the KING- don't settle for junk.
Partake of the riches He
has for you.

◊

DON'T GIVE UP ON GOD!

◊

Live *peaceably* with all men. *Roman 12:18*

◊

A doubled-minded man is unstable in all his ways.
James 1:8

Inspired to Inspire

Worry does not empty tomorrow of its trouble. It empties today of its strength.

◊

Wisdom, like an inheritance, is a good thing.

Psalm 7:11

◊

A true friend is someone who reaches for your hand and touches your heart.

◊

Nehemiah teaches us three important truths about handling criticism:

◊

1. Expect it
2. Evaluate it
3. Outlive it

Inspired to Inspire

I am not afraid of *tomorrow* for I have seen *yesterday* and I love *today.*

◊

Focus and all else becomes clear.

◊

Everyone can't be in your front row.

◊

Pruning allows growth to take place
-Shed the dead weight.

◊

A successful man continues to look for work after he has found a job.

Inspired to Inspire

You are light in the Lord. Walk as children of light.
Ephesians 5:8

◊

Pray without Ceasing. I Thessalonians 5:17

◊

If you are not criticized, you may not be doing much.

Donald H. Rumsfeld

◊

Common sense is priceless!

◊

The Best Antique is an Old Friend.

Inspired to Inspire

Don't always blame others for your problems-examine yourself to see what part you played.

◊

REVIEW- REDO-REVIEW

◊

It is for us to pray not for tasks equal to our powers, but for powers equal to our tasks. Helen Keller

◊

Surely goodness and mercy shall follow me all the days of my life;

and I will dwell in the house of the Lord forever. Psalm 23:6

◊

If you just sit there..... Will Rogers

Inspired to Inspire

"We all carry a responsibility to do what we can when it will make a difference."

Michael Useem, Leading Up

◊

**The true Meaning of LIFE is to plant trees, under whose shade you do not expect to sit.
Nelson Henderson**

◊

**Failure is success if we learn from it.
Malcolm Forbes**

◊

Wake Up with a mind to make positive choices today you deserves the best!

Inspired to Inspire

You can complain because roses have thorns,
or you can rejoice because thorns have roses.

ZIGGY

◊

Action may not always bring happiness; but there is no happiness without action. Benjamin Disraeli

◊

Write the Vision, and make it plain upon tables,
that he that read it may run.

◊

<u>Success seems to be largely a matter of hanging on after others have let go.</u>
William Feather

◊

You can accomplish much if you don't care who gets the credit. Ronald Reagan

Inspired to Inspire

Ability may take you to the top but it
takes character to keep you there.
John Wooden

◊

The World is a dangerous place, not because

of the people who are evil, but because

of the people who don't do anything about it.

Albert Einstein

*The Pessimist Complains About The Wind; The Optimist
Expects It To Change; The Realist Adjust The Sails.
William Arthur Ward*

◊

**Everyone thinks of changing the world, but no one thinks of
changing himself. Leo Nikolaevich Tolstoy**

Inspired to Inspire

"If I had My Life to Live Over"
By Erma Bombeck

If I had my life to live over again, I would have waxed less and listened more.

◊

Instead of wishing away nine months of pregnancy and complaining about the shadow over my feet, I'd have cherished every minute of it and realized that the wonderment of growing inside me was to be my only chance in life to assist God is a miracle.

I would never have insisted the car windows be rolled up on a summer day because my hair had been teased and sprayed.

I would have invited my friends over to dinner even if the carpet was stained and the sofa faded.

I would have eaten popcorn in the "good" living room and worried less about the dirt when you lit the fireplace.

I would have taken the time to listen to my grandfather ramble about his youth.

Inspired to Inspire

I would have sat cross-legged on the lawn with my children and never worried about grass stains.

I would have cried and laughed less while watching television- and more while watching real life.

I would have shared more of the responsibility carried by my husband.

I would have eaten less cottage cheese and more ice cream.

I would have gone to bed when I was sick instead of pretending the Earth would go into a holding pattern if I weren't there for a day.

I would never have bought anything just because it was practical, wouldn't show soil, or was guaranteed to last a lifetime.

◊

When my child kissed me impetuously, I would never have said, "Later. Now, go get washed up for dinner."

Inspired to Inspire

There would have been more I love yous, more I'm sorrys, more I'm listenings, but mostly, given another shot at life, I would seize every minute of it, look at it and really

see it.. try it on.. exhaust it...and never give that minute back until there was nothing left of it.

◊

A lot of people mistake a short memory

for a clear conscience

◊

Now unto Him that is able to keep you from falling, and to present you faultless before the presence of his glory with exceeding joy,

◊

To the only wise God our Saviour, be glory and majesty,
dominion and power, both now and ever,
Amen
Jude 1:24-25

Inspired to Inspire

Life is 10% what happens to you and 90% how you react.

◊

Great work is done by people who are not afraid to be great.
Fernando Flores

◊

Keep On Living ~ cause after this is your VICTORY!~ Clarissa Pace

◊

DON'T WORRY -THE POLICY HAS NOT CHANGE- JESUS IS STILL LORD AND HIS WORD WILL NEVER FAIL

◊

God is not like cops, He allows U-turns.

Inspired to Inspire

Although the sun is not shining outside,

the SON can be shining on the inside.

◊

Make haters your Motivators

◊

Give your words an assignment- Rod Parsley

◊

Hard work spotlights the character of people: some turn up their sleeves, some turn up their noses, and some don't turn up at all. Sam Ewing

◊

*Give the best you have, and it will never be enough-Give your best anyway.
Mother Teresa*

Inspired to Inspire

Learn how to be happy with what you have

while you pursue all that you want

Jim Rohn

◊

And I will restore to you the years that the *locust*

hath eaten, the *cankerworm*, and the caterpillar, and the

PALMERWORM.

Joel 2:25

◊

Don't let your negative perception become a reality.

◊

The GRAND essentials to happiness in this life are something to do, something to love and something to hope for.

Inspired to Inspire

HOPE
IS
Holding On Preparing for an EXIT

◊

We Walk by faith- not by SIGHT

◊

Neither give place to the devil. Ephesian 4:27

◊

Death and life are in the power of the tongue; and they that love it shall eat the fruit thereof.
Proverbs 18:21

◊

Listening! You will come to appreciate the art one day.

Inspired to Inspire

When thou liest down, thou shalt not be afraid: yea, thou shalt lie down, and thy sleep shall be sweet. Proverbs 3:24

◊

Don't let what supposed to be a trip turn into a journey.

◊

What matters is not faith and works; it is not faith or works; it is faith that works.

◊

Whatsoever things are true, whatsoever things are honest, whatsoever things are just, whatsoever things are pure, whatsoever things are lovely, whatsoever things are of good report; if there be any virtue, and if there be any praise, think on these things.
Philippians 4:8

◊

Don't be afraid to say, " I need help."

Inspired to Inspire

I declare that I am created for GOOD works.

◊

Be not *deceived;* God is not **MOCKED:** for whatsoever a man *soweth,* that shall he also reap.
Galatians 6:7

◊

"How far you go in life depends on your being tender with the young, compassionate with the aged, sympathetic with the striving and tolerant of the weak and strong. Because someday in your life you will have been all of these."

George Washington Carver

Inspired to Inspire

Figure it out for yourself, my lad.
You've all that the greatest of men have had,
Two arms, two hands, two legs, two eyes
And a brain to use if you would be wise.
With this equipment they all began,
So start for the top and say, 'I can.'

Edgar A. Guest

◊

Let nothing be done through strife or vainglory; but in
lowliness of mind let each esteem others
better than themselves.
Philippians 2:3

◊

DON'T EXPECT OTHERS TO LISTEN TO
YOUR ADVICE AND
IGNORE YOUR EXAMPLE

Inspired to Inspire

Finish each day and be done with it. You have done what you could; some blunders and absurdities have crept in; forget them as soon as you can. Tomorrow is a new day; you shall begin it serenely and with too high a spirit to be encumbered with your old nonsense.

Ralph Waldo Emerson

◊

*"In matters of style, swim with the current;
in matters of principle, stand like a rock."
Thomas Jefferson*

◊

It shall come to pass, that before they call, I will answer, and while they are yet speaking, I will hear. Isaiah 65:24 KJV

◊

Inspired to Inspire

About the Author

Lou E. Lambert, the oldest of six children was born in Grapevine, Ar, on the Grant end of Princeton Pipe, in the Bookman Community between Pine Bluff and Sheridan – a place where everybody knows your name, to the late John Samuel James and Essie Lee James.

Lou was reared in a home where encouragement was a household word, thus giving her the fuel to ignite in whatever area she desired to pursue.

She was educated in the Grapevine schools and later received a BS Degree in Education from the University of Arkansas at Monticello. As a teacher, she gave back to her community by teaching three years for the Grapevine Public School District.

She has since been employed for the last 22 1/2 years with the Arkansas Department of Human Services.

She is married to James Carl Lambert of Monticello. She is a mother and a grandmother. She is a member of Revival Center Church of God in Christ, where she serves under the leadership of Supt. Michael A. Jones in the 3rd Jurisdiction of Arkansas. She is a license Evangelist-Missionary, a member of the Trustee Board, Sunday School Superinten-

Inspired to Inspire

dent, Usher Board President and serves in other ministry areas within her local, district and state churches.

She recognizes and seizes the opportunity to inspire those who she comes in contact with daily. One of her favorite quotes is "Life is a just employer. He will give you what you ask, but once you have set the wages, you must then bear the task."

Made in the USA
Columbia, SC
07 February 2025